Dear Parent:
Your child's love of reading starts here!

Every child learns to read in a different way and at his or her own speed. Some go back and forth between reading levels and read favorite books again and again. Others read through each level in order. You can help your young reader improve and become more confident by encouraging his or her own interests and abilities. From books your child reads with you to the first books he or she reads alone, there are I Can Read Books for every stage of reading:

SHARED READING
Basic language, word repetition, and whimsical illustrations, ideal for sharing with your emergent reader

BEGINNING READING
Short sentences, familiar words, and simple concepts for children eager to read on their own

READING WITH HELP
Engaging stories, longer sentences, and language play for developing readers

READING ALONE
Complex plots, challenging vocabulary, and high-interest topics for the independent reader

ADVANCED READING
Short paragraphs, chapters, and exciting themes for the perfect bridge to chapter books

I Can Read Books have introduced children to the joy of reading since 1957. Featuring award-winning authors and illustrators and a fabulous cast of beloved characters, I Can Read Books set the standard for beginning readers.

A lifetime of discovery begins with the magical words "I Can Read!"

Visit www.icanread.com for information
on enriching your child's reading experience.

Hamsters, Shells, and Spelling Bees
School Poems

edited by
Lee Bennett Hopkins
pictures by Sachiko Yoshikawa

HarperCollinsPublishers

Acknowledgments

Thanks are due to the following for use of works that appear in this collection:

Boyds Mills Press for "Not Fair" from *Somebody Catch My Homework* by David L. Harrison. Copyright © 1993 by David L. Harrison. Reprinted by permission.

Curtis Brown, Ltd., for "Backpack Buddy" and "Ready" by Rebecca Kai Dotlich; copyright © 2008 by Rebecca Kai Dotlich. "My Teacher" by Lee Bennett Hopkins; copyright © 2008 by Lee Bennett Hopkins. "Maps" by Jane Yolen; copyright © 2008 by Jane Yolen. All reprinted by permission of Curtis Brown, Ltd.

Sandra Gilbert Brüg for "Listening." Used by permission of the author, who controls all rights.

Chetra Kotzas for "Lunch Bag." Used by permission of the author, who controls all rights.

Linda Kulp for "True Love." Used by permission of the author, who controls all rights.

J. Patrick Lewis for "Library" and "School Bus Driver." Used by permission of the author, who controls all rights.

Meadowbrook Press for "Measles" from *No More Homework! No More Tests!* by Bruce Lansky. Copyright © 1997 by Bruce Lansky. Reprinted with permission of Meadowbrook Press.

Leslie Danford Perkins for "Art Class." Used by permission of the author, who controls all rights.

Louis Phillips for "The Eraser Poem." Used by permission of the author, who controls all rights.

Heidi Bee Roemer for "Spelling Bee." Used by permission of the author, who controls all rights.

Alice Schertle for "Question." Used by permission of the author, who controls all rights.

Janet Settimo for "Hamster Math." Used by permission of the author, who controls all rights.

Ann Rousseau Smith for "Buzz." Used by permission of the author, who controls all rights.

Elizabeth Upton for "Show and Tell." Used by permission of the author, who controls all rights.

Amy Ludwig VanDerwater for "School Play." Used by permission of the author, who controls all rights.

Sharon Vargo for "Looking Through the Microscope." Used by permission of the author, who controls all rights.

Hamsters, Shells, and Spelling Bees: School Poems Text copyright © 2008 by Lee Bennett Hopkins Illustrations copyright © 2008 by Sachiko Yoshikawa All rights reserved. No part of this book may be used or reproduced in any manner whatsoever without written permission except in the case of brief quotations embodied in critical articles and reviews. Printed in the United States of America. For information address HarperCollins Children's Books, a division of HarperCollins Publishers, 1350 Avenue of the Americas, New York, NY 10019. www.harpercollinschildrens.com

Library of Congress Cataloging-in-Publication Data

Hopkins, Lee Bennett.
   Hamsters, shells, and spelling bees : school poems / edited by Lee Bennett Hopkins ; pictures by Sachiko Yoshikawa.— 1st ed.
     p. cm. — (An I can read book)
   ISBN 978-0-06-074112-9 (trade bdg.)
   ISBN 978-0-06-074113-6 (lib. bdg.)
   I. Schools—Poetry. II. Title. III. Series.
PS595.S34 H36 2007   2007020881
811/.608—dc22   CIP
                                      AC

1 2 3 4 5 6 7 8 9 10   ❖   First Edition

To my great-niece
Erin Elizabeth Bice
—L.B.H.

For Takako Hayakawa,
with special thanks to Namiko Rudi
—S.Y.

Contents

Ready
by Rebecca Kai Dotlich

Stars sleep as I wake

to this brand-new school day

ready

to

smile.

9

Hamster Math

by Janet Settimo

I'm taking back these hamsters

I've kept all summer long.

I had no way of knowing

That something would go wrong.

When Teacher gave me Sam and Max,

Two furry, friendly guys,

She never guessed they'd multiply

Before my very eyes.

I had hamsters on my dresser,

And hamsters in my drawer,

Hamsters on the windowsill,

And hamsters on the floor.

They were adding and dividing,

Multiplying by the score,

I never knew that one plus one

Could total twenty-four!

School Bus Driver
by J. Patrick Lewis

I hear the engine rumbling

As she sits out by the street,

Waiting for a slowpoke *(me!)*

To climb into his seat.

I don't know how she does it
Every day at 8:03,
Bur rain or snow or sleet I know
She's always there for me.

Backpack Buddy
by Rebecca Kai Dotlich

Zip it up. Off I ride,

everything I need inside . . .

sack of lunch, a permission note,

library books, a poem I wrote,

markers, folder, sticker stars,

a word list for our spelling bee . . .

Zip it up. Off I ride.

My backpack buddy and me.

My Teacher
by Lee Bennett Hopkins

My teacher

loves

reading books aloud

putting up new bulletin boards

taking vacations by the sea

but—

best of all

my teacher

loves

ME.

17

Show and Tell
by Elizabeth Upton

My shell

makes sounds

of waves rushing and crashing.

Somehow it saved up

seashore sounds

when it lived on the beach.

Do you want to hear

its ocean song?

Go ahead,

listen to my shell.

Maps
by Jane Yolen

We are making maps:

maps of our classroom,

maps of our school,

maps of our town.

We let our fingers walk

the straight lines

from window to door,

down school hallways

that gently curve,

along town streets

as crooked as question marks.

We trace old rail lines,

the bumps of mountains,

a blue swirl of river,

the broad turnpike lanes.

You can walk like that all day

and never get tired.

Looking Through the Microscope

by Sharon Vargo

I zoom in.

I zoom out.

Secret places
hidden spaces
captured by
a magic eye . . .

a tiny world
magnified.

Art Class
by Leslie Danford Perkins

Dream catchers hanging

with feathers and beads.

Pictures from popping corn,

lentils and seeds.

Egg carton centipedes,
paintings with sand.
Art is a feast for
my eyes and my hands.

Library
by J. Patrick Lewis

Come right in,

Look around

At all the treasures

That are bound

To make you glad

For a week or two

Until your treasure's

Overdue.

26

Listening

by Sandra Gilbert Brüg

I like to hear my teacher's voice

when she reads out loud

in our story nook.

Her voice

brings magical sounds

to each new character.

I sit close to my friends
on a fuzzy red rug—
like one big family

listening . . . loving
this book.

Lunch Bag
by Chetra Kotzas

Bulging

brown paper bag

hiding

one peanut butter sandwich,

round cookies,

chocolate and chipped,

sweet bubbly pineapple juice

    with a twisty silver cap—

and

a little note that says:

    I LOVE YOU.

    GUESS WHO?

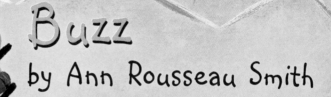

Buzz
by Ann Rousseau Smith

Buzz . . .

Inside our classroom
Zooms a bee.
It zips, dips,
Tries to flee.

Buzz . . .

As students duck
And papers fly,
The whizzing bee
Comes racing by.

Buzz . . .

It zigzags back

Above the floor.

At last it finds

An open door.

Buzzzzzz . . .

Not Fair
by David L. Harrison

Sitting in school

On an April day

Isn't fair.

A guy should be flying

A kite with the wind

In his hair.

I know I'm supposed

To be doing my math,

I don't care.

Sitting in school

On an April day

Isn't fair.

Question
by Alice Schertle

Pencil stub, I must

ask myself: How many more

poems are in you?

37

The Eraser Poem
by Louis Phillips

The eraser poem

The eraser poe

The eraser po

The eraser p

The eraser

The erase

The eras

The era

The er

The e

The

Th

T

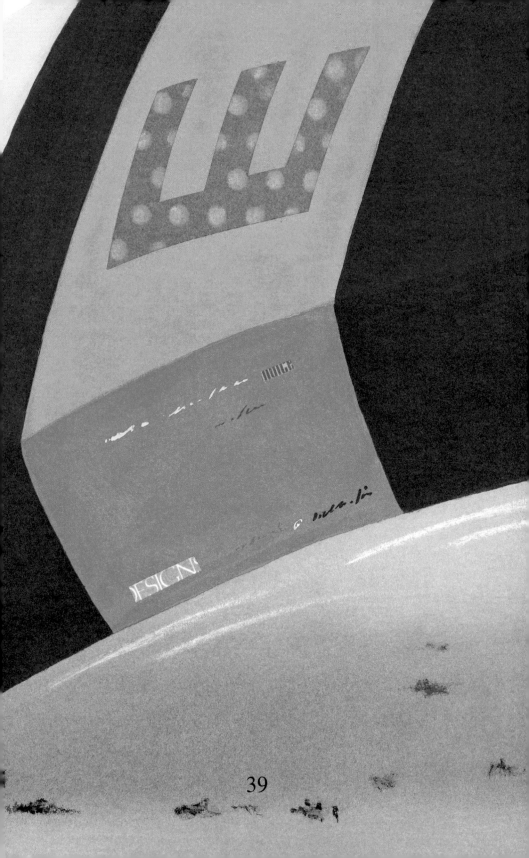

Measles
by Bruce Lansky

There are measles on my forehead.

There are measles on my nose.

There are measles on my elbows.

There are measles on my toes.

There are measles on the carpet.

There are measles on the chair.

There are measles on my glasses.

There are measles in my hair.

Calendar

I'm so tired of painting measles.

I would like to take a rest.

I sure hope that I look sick enough

to miss tomorrow's test.

Spelling Bee
by Heidi Bee Roemer

Knees knocking.

Heart pounding.

I hear my teacher say,

  "*TARANTULA.*"

I spell the word.

I got it right!

Hip,

  hip,

    hip,

      hooray!

43

School Play
by Amy Ludwig VanDerwater

A stage

with velvet curtains

is tucked inside my heart

where you can find me

in my costume

practicing my part

every night—

every day.

I *will*
be ready
for our play.

True Love
by Linda Kulp

Every day

after school

my cat sits

on the windowsill

waiting,

watching

for me

to come home

from school.

I open

the door

to her

purr-ing.

Index of Authors and Titles